Acclaim for *A Small Place*

"A loving explanation . . . a small book full of big ideas."
—*New York Newsday*

"This is truth, beautifully and powerfully stated . . . In truly lyrical language that makes you read aloud, [Kincaid] takes you from the dizzying blue of the Caribbean to the sewage of hotels and clubs where black Antiguans are only allowed to work . . . Truth, wisdom, insight, outrage, and cutting wit."   —*The Atlanta Journal-Constitution*

"Like 'The Ancient Mariner' in Coleridge's poem, Kincaid will not let you go until you've heard her tale."
—*Boston Herald*

"Wonderful reading . . . Tells more about the Caribbean in 80 pages than all the guidebooks."
—*The Philadelphia Inquirer*

"Intimate . . . emotional . . . beautifully written."
—*The Virginian-Pilot*

Jamaica Kincaid
A Small Place

Jamaica Kincaid was born in St. John's, Antigua. Her books include *At the Bottom of the River*, *Annie John*, *Lucy*, *The Autobiography of My Mother*, *My Brother*, *My Favorite Plant*, and *My Garden (Book):*. She lives with her family in Vermont.

Also by **Jamaica Kincaid**

At the Bottom of the River

Annie John

Lucy

The Autobiography of My Mother

My Brother

My Favorite Plant (editor)

My Garden (Book):

A Small Place

A SMALL PLACE

Jamaica Kincaid

Farrar, Straus and Giroux
New York

Farrar, Straus and Giroux
18 West 18th Street, New York 10011

Distributed in Canada by Douglas & McIntyre Ltd.
Printed in the United States of America
Published in 1988 by Farrar, Straus and Giroux
First Farrar, Straus and Giroux paperback edition, 2000

The author wishes to express her gratitude to the John Simon Guggenheim
Foundation for its generous support during the writing of this book.

The Library of Congress has cataloged the hardcover edition as follows:
Kincaid, Jamaica.
    A small place / Jamaica Kincaid.— 1st ed.
    p. cm.
    ISBN-13: 978-0-374-26638-7
    ISBN-10: 0-374-26638-7
    1. Kincaid, Jamaica—Homes and haunts—Antigua and Barbuda—Antigua.
2. Novelists, Antiguan—Biography.   3. Antigua—Description and travel.
4. Antigua—Intellectual life—20th century.   I. Title.

F2035 .K56 1988
972.92—dc19

                                                           88000376

Paperback ISBN-13: 978-0-374-52707-5
Paperback ISBN-10: 0-374-52707-5

Designed by Cynthia Krupat

www.fsgbooks.com

28   30   29

For Brian and Veronica Dyde;
for my brothers
Joseph, Dalma, and Devon Drew
with love;
and for William Shawn (again)
with gratitude and love

IF YOU GO to Antigua as a tourist, this is what you will see. If you come by aeroplane, you will land at the V. C. Bird International Airport. Vere Cornwall (V. C.) Bird is the Prime Minister of Antigua. You may be the sort of tourist who would wonder why a Prime Minister would want an airport named after him—why not a school, why not a hospital, why not some great public monument? You are a tourist and you have not yet seen a school in Antigua, you have not yet seen the hospital in Antigua, you have not yet seen a public monument in Antigua. As your plane descends to land, you might say, What a beautiful island Antigua is— more beautiful than any of the other islands you have seen, and they were very beautiful, in their way, but they were much too green, much too lush with vegetation, which indicated to you, the tourist, that they got quite a bit of rainfall, and rain is the very thing that you, just now, do not want, for you are thinking of the hard and cold and dark and long days you spent working in North America (or, worse, Europe), earning some money so that you could stay in this place (Antigua) where the sun always shines and where the climate is deliciously hot and dry for the four to ten days you are going to be staying there; and since you are on your holiday, since you are a tourist, the thought of what it might be like for someone who had to live day in, day out in a place that suffers constantly from drought, and so has to watch carefully every drop of fresh water used (while at the same time surrounded by a sea and an ocean—the Caribbean Sea on one side, the Atlantic Ocean on the other), must never cross your mind.

You disembark from your plane. You go through customs. Since you are a tourist, a North American or European—to be frank, white—and not an Antiguan black returning to Antigua from Europe or North America with cardboard boxes of much needed cheap clothes and food for relatives, you move through customs swiftly, you move through customs with ease. Your bags are not searched. You emerge from customs into the hot, clean air: immediately you feel cleansed, immediately you feel blessed (which is to say special); you feel free. You see a man, a taxi driver; you ask him to take you to your destination; he quotes you a price. You immediately think that the price is in the local currency, for you are a tourist and you are familiar with these things (rates of exchange) and you feel even more free, for things seem so cheap, but then your driver ends by saying, "In U.S. currency." You may say, "Hmmmm, do you have a formal sheet that lists official prices and destinations?" Your driver obeys the law and shows you the sheet, and he apologises for the incredible mistake he has made in quoting you a price off the top of his head which is so vastly different (favouring him) from the one listed. You are driven to your hotel by this taxi driver in his taxi, a brand-new Japanese-made vehicle. The road on which you are travelling is a very bad road, very much in need of repair. You are feeling wonderful, so you say, "Oh, what a marvellous change these bad roads are from the splendid highways I am used to in North America." (Or, worse, Europe.) Your driver is reckless; he is a dangerous man who drives in the middle of the road when he thinks no other cars are coming in the opposite direction, passes other cars on blind curves that run uphill, drives at sixty miles an hour on narrow, curving roads when the road sign, a rusting, beat-up thing left over from colonial days, says 40 MPH. This might frighten you (you are on your holiday; you are a tourist); this might excite you (you are on your holiday; you are a tourist), though if you are from New York and take taxis you are used to this style of driving: most of the taxi drivers in New York are from places in the world like this. You are looking out the window (because you want to get your money's worth); you notice that all the cars you see are brand-new, or almost brand-new, and that they are all Japanese-made. There are no American cars in Antigua—no new ones, at any rate; none that were manufactured in the last ten years. You continue to look at the cars and you say to yourself, Why, they look brand-new, but they have an awful sound, like an old car—a very old, dilapidated car. How to account for that? Well, possibly it's because they use leaded gasoline in these brand-new cars whose engines were built to use non-leaded gasoline, but you musn't ask the person driving the car if this is so, because he or she has never heard of unleaded gasoline. You look closely at the car; you see that it's a model of a Japanese car that you might hesitate to buy; it's a model that's very expensive; it's a model that's quite impractical for a person who has to work as hard as you do and who watches every penny you earn so that you can afford this holiday you are on. How do they afford such a car? And do they live in a luxurious house to match such a car? Well, no. You will be surprised, then, to see that most likely the person driving this brand-new car filled with the wrong gas lives in a house that, in comparison, is far beneath the status of the car; and if you were to ask why you would be told that the banks are encouraged by the government to make loans available for cars, but loans for houses not so easily available; and if you ask again why, you will be told that the two main car dealerships in Antigua are owned in part or outright by ministers in government. Oh, but you are on holiday and the sight of these brand-new cars driven by people who may or may not have really passed their driving test (there was once a scandal about driving licences for sale) would not really stir up these thoughts in you. You pass a building sitting in a sea of dust and you think, It's some latrines for people just passing by, but when you look again you see the building has written on it PIGOTT'S SCHOOL. You pass the hospital, the Holberton Hospital, and how wrong you are not to think about this, for though you are a tourist on your holiday, what if your heart should miss a few beats? What if a blood vessel in your neck should break? What if one of those people driving those brand-new cars filled with the wrong gas fails to pass safely while going uphill on a curve and you are in the car going in the opposite direction? Will you be comforted to know that the hospital is staffed with doctors that no actual Antiguan trusts; that Antiguans always say about the doctors, "I don't want them near me"; that Antiguans refer to them not as doctors but as "the three men" (there are three of them); that when the Minister of Health himself doesn't feel well he takes the first plane to New York to see a real doctor; that if any one of the ministers in government needs medical care he flies to New York to get it?

It's a good thing that you brought your own books with you, for you couldn't just go to the library and borrow some. Antigua used to have a splendid library, but in The Earthquake (everyone talks about it that way—The Earthquake; we Antiguans, for I am one, have a great sense of things, and the more meaningful the thing, the more meaningless we make it) the library building was damaged. This was in 1974, and soon after that a sign was placed on the front of the building

saying, THIS BUILDING WAS DAMAGED IN THE EARTH-
QUAKE OF 1974. REPAIRS ARE PENDING. The sign
hangs there, and hangs there more than a decade
later, with its unfulfilled promise of repair, and you
might see this as a sort of quaintness on the part
of these islanders, these people descended from
slaves—what a strange, unusual perception of time
they have. REPAIRS ARE PENDING, and here it is
many years later, but perhaps in a world that is
twelve miles long and nine miles wide (the size of
Antigua) twelve years and twelve minutes and
twelve days are all the same. The library is one of
those splendid old buildings from colonial times,
and the sign telling of the repairs is a splendid old
sign from colonial times. Not very long after The
Earthquake Antigua got its independence from Britain, making Antigua a state in its own right, and
Antiguans are so proud of this that each year, to
mark the day, they go to church and thank God,
a British God, for this. But you should not think of
the confusion that must lie in all that and you must
not think of the damaged library. You have brought
your own books with you, and among them is one
of those new books about economic history, one of
those books explaining how the West (meaning
Europe and North America after its conquest and
settlement by Europeans) got rich: the West got

rich not from the free (free—in this case meaning got-for-nothing) and then undervalued labour, for generations, of the people like me you see walking around you in Antigua but from the ingenuity of small shopkeepers in Sheffield and Yorkshire and Lancashire, or wherever; and what a great part the invention of the wristwatch played in it, for there was nothing noble-minded men could not do when they discovered they could slap time on their wrists just like that (isn't that the last straw; for not only did we have to suffer the unspeakableness of slavery, but the satisfaction to be had from "We made you bastards rich" is taken away, too), and so you needn't let that slightly funny feeling you have from time to time about exploitation, oppression, domination develop into full-fledged unease, discomfort; you could ruin your holiday. They are not responsible for what you have; you owe them nothing; in fact, you did them a big favour, and you can provide one hundred examples. For here you are now, passing by Government House. And here you are now, passing by the Prime Minister's Office and the Parliament Building, and overlooking these, with a splendid view of St. John's Harbour, the American Embassy. If it were not for you, they would not have Government House, and Prime Minister's Office, and Parliament Building and

embassy of powerful country. Now you are passing a mansion, an extraordinary house painted the
colour of old cow dung, with more aerials and an-
tennas attached to it than you will see even at the
American Embassy. The people who live in this
house are a merchant family who came to Antigua
from the Middle East less than twenty years ago.
When this family first came to Antigua, they sold
dry goods door to door from suitcases they carried
on their backs. Now they own a lot of Antigua;
they regularly lend money to the government, they
build enormous (for Antigua), ugly (for Antigua),
concrete buildings in Antigua's capital, St. John's,
which the government then rents for huge sums of
money; a member of their family is the Antiguan
Ambassador to Syria; Antiguans hate them. Not
far from this mansion is another mansion, the home
of a drug smuggler. Everybody knows he's a drug
smuggler, and if just as you were driving by he
stepped out of his door your driver might point him
out to you as the notorious person that he is, for
this drug smuggler is so rich people say he buys
cars in tens—ten of this one, ten of that one—and
that he bought a house (another mansion) near
Five Islands, contents included, with cash he carried
in a suitcase: three hundred and fifty thousand
American dollars, and, to the surprise of the seller

of the house, lots of American dollars were left over. Overlooking the drug smuggler's mansion is yet another mansion, and leading up to it is the best paved road in all of Antigua—even better than the road that was paved for the Queen's visit in 1985 (when the Queen came, all the roads that she would travel on were paved anew, so that the Queen might have been left with the impression that riding in a car in Antigua was a pleasant experience). In this mansion lives a woman sophisticated people in Antigua call Evita. She is a notorious woman. She's young and beautiful and the girlfriend of somebody very high up in the government. Evita is notorious because her relationship with this high government official has made her the owner of boutiques and property and given her a say in cabinet meetings, and all sorts of other privileges such a relationship would bring a beautiful young woman.

Oh, but by now you are tired of all this looking, and you want to reach your destination—your hotel, your room. You long to refresh yourself; you long to eat some nice lobster, some nice local food. You take a bath, you brush your teeth. You get dressed again; as you get dressed, you look out the window. That water—have you ever seen anything like it? Far out, to the horizon, the colour of the water is navy-blue; nearer, the water is the colour of the North American sky. From there to the shore, the water is pale, silvery, clear, so clear that you can see its pinkish-white sand bottom. Oh, what beauty! Oh, what beauty! You have never seen anything like this. You are so excited. You breathe shallow. You breathe deep. You see a beautiful boy skimming the water, godlike, on a Windsurfer. You see an incredibly unattractive, fat, pastrylike-fleshed woman enjoying a walk on the beautiful sand, with a man, an incredibly unattractive, fat, pastrylike-fleshed man; you see the pleasure they're taking in their surroundings. Still standing, looking out the window, you see yourself lying on the beach, enjoying the amazing sun (a sun so powerful and yet so beautiful, the way it is always overhead as if on permanent guard, ready to stamp out any cloud that dares to darken and so empty rain on you and ruin your holiday; a sun that is your personal friend). You see yourself taking a walk on that beach, you see yourself meeting new people (only they are new in a very limited way, for they are people just like you). You see yourself eating some delicious, locally grown food. You see yourself, you see yourself . . . You must not wonder what exactly happened to the contents of your lavatory when you flushed it. You must not wonder where your bathwater went when you pulled out the stopper. You must not wonder what happened when you brushed your teeth. Oh, it might all end up in the water you are thinking of taking a swim in; the contents of your lavatory might, just might, graze gently against your ankle as you wade carefree in the water, for you see, in Antigua, there is no proper sewage-disposal system. But the Caribbean Sea is very big and the Atlantic Ocean is even bigger; it would amaze even you to know the number of black slaves this ocean has swallowed up. When you sit down to eat your delicious meal, it's better that you don't know that most of what you are eating came off a plane from Miami. And before it got on a plane in Miami, who knows where it came from? A good guess is that it came from a place like Antigua first, where it was grown dirt-cheap, went to Miami, and came back. There is a world of something in this, but I can't go into it right now.

The thing you have always suspected about yourself the minute you become a tourist is true: A tourist is an ugly human being. You are not an ugly person all the time; you are not an ugly person ordinarily; you are not an ugly person day to day. From day to day, you are a nice person. From day

to day, all the people who are supposed to love you
on the whole do. From day to day, as you walk down
a busy street in the large and modern and prosperous city in which you work and live, dismayed,
puzzled (a cliché, but only a cliché can explain
you) at how alone you feel in this crowd, how
awful it is to go unnoticed, how awful it is to go
unloved, even as you are surrounded by more people
than you could possibly get to know in a lifetime
that lasted for millennia, and then out of the corner
of your eye you see someone looking at you and
absolute pleasure is written all over that person's
face, and then you realise that you are not as re-
volting a presence as you think you are (for that
look just told you so). And so, ordinarily, you are
a nice person, an attractive person, a person capable
of drawing to yourself the affection of other people
(people just like you), a person at home in your
own skin (sort of; I mean, in a way; I mean, your
dismay and puzzlement are natural to you, because
people like you just seem to be like that, and so
many of the things people like you find admirable
about yourselves—the things you think about, the
things you think really define you—seem rooted in
these feelings): a person at home in your own
house (and all its nice house things), with its nice
back yard (and its nice back-yard things), at home

on your street, your church, in community activities, your job, at home with your family, your relatives, your friends—you are a whole person. But one day, when you are sitting somewhere, alone in that crowd, and that awful feeling of displacedness comes over you, and really, as an ordinary person you are not well equipped to look too far inward and set yourself aright, because being ordinary is already so taxing, and being ordinary takes all you have out of you, and though the words "I must get away" do not actually pass across your lips, you make a leap from being that nice blob just sitting like a boob in your amniotic sac of the modern experience to being a person visiting heaps of death and ruin and feeling alive and inspired at the sight of it; to being a person lying on some faraway beach, your stilled body stinking and glistening in the sand, looking like something first forgotten, then remembered, then not important enough to go back for; to being a person marvelling at the harmony (ordinarily, what you would say is the backwardness) and the union these other people (and they are other people) have with nature. And you look at the things they can do with a piece of ordinary cloth, the things they fashion out of cheap, vulgarly colored (to you) twine, the way they squat down over a hole they have made in the ground, the hole itself is something to marvel at, and since you are being an ugly person this ugly but joyful thought will swell inside you: their ancestors were not clever in the way yours were and not ruthless in the way yours were, for then would it not be you who would be in harmony with nature and backwards in that charming way? An ugly thing, that is what you are when you become a tourist, an ugly, empty thing, a stupid thing, a piece of rubbish pausing here and there to gaze at this and taste that, and it will never occur to you that the people who inhabit the place in which you have just paused cannot stand you, that behind their closed doors they laugh at your strangeness (you do not look the way they look); the physical sight of you does not please them; you have bad manners (it is their custom to eat their food with their hands; you try eating their way, you look silly; you try eating the way you always eat, you look silly); they do not like the way you speak (you have an accent); they collapse helpless from laughter, mimicking the way they imagine you must look as you carry out some everyday bodily function. They do not like you. *They do not like me!* That thought never actually occurs to you. Still, you feel a little uneasy. Still, you feel a little foolish. Still, you feel a little out of place. But the banality of your own life is very real to you; it drove you to this extreme, spending your days and your nights in the company of people who despise you, people you do not like really, people you would not want to have as your actual neighbour. And so you must devote yourself to puzzling out how much of what you are told is really, really true (Is ground-up bottle glass in peanut sauce really a delicacy around here, or will it do just what you think ground-up bottle glass will do? Is this rare, multicoloured, snout-mouthed fish really an aphrodisiac, or will it cause you to fall asleep permanently?). Oh, the hard work all of this is, and is it any wonder, then, that on your return home you feel the need of a long rest, so that you can recover from your life as a tourist?

That the native does not like the tourist is not hard to explain. For every native of every place is a potential tourist, and every tourist is a native of somewhere. Every native everywhere lives a life of overwhelming and crushing banality and boredom and desperation and depression, and every deed, good and bad, is an attempt to forget this. Every native would like to find a way out, every native would like a rest, every native would like a tour. But some natives—most natives in the world— cannot go anywhere. They are too poor. They are too poor to go anywhere. They are too poor to escape the reality of their lives; and they are too poor to live properly in the place where they live, which is the very place you, the tourist, want to go—so when the natives see you, the tourist, they envy you, they envy your ability to leave your own banality and boredom, they envy your ability to turn their own banality and boredom into a source of pleasure for yourself.

THE ANTIGUA that I knew, the Antigua in which I grew up, is not the Antigua you, a tourist, would see now. That Antigua no longer exists. That Antigua no longer exists partly for the usual reason, the passing of time, and partly because the bad-minded people who used to rule over it, the English, no longer do so. (But the English have become such a pitiful lot these days, with hardly any idea what to do with themselves now that they no longer have one quarter of the earth's human population bowing and scraping before them. They don't seem to know that this empire business was all wrong and they should, at least, be wearing sackcloth and ashes in token penance of the wrongs committed, the irrevocableness of their bad deeds, for no natural disaster imaginable could equal the harm they did. Actual death might have been better. And so all this fuss over empire—what went wrong here, what went wrong there—always makes me quite crazy, for I can say to them what went wrong: they should never have left their home, their precious England, a place they loved so much, a place they had to leave but could never forget. And so everywhere they went they turned it into England; and everybody they met they turned English. But no place could ever really be England, and nobody who did not look exactly like them would ever be English, so you can imagine the destruction of people and land that came from that. The English hate each other and they hate England, and the reason they are so miserable now is that they have no place else to go and nobody else to feel better than.) But let me show you the Antigua that I used to know.

In the Antigua that I knew, we lived on a street named after an English maritime criminal, Horatio Nelson, and all the other streets around us were named after some other English maritime criminals. There was Rodney Street, there was Hood Street, there was Hawkins Street, and there was Drake Street. There were flamboyant trees and mahogany trees lining East Street. Government House, the place where the Governor, the person standing in for the Queen, lived, was on East Street. Government House was surrounded by a high white wall—and to show how cowed we must have been, no one ever wrote bad things on it; it remained clean and white and high. (I once stood in hot sun for hours so that I could see a putty-faced Princess from England disappear behind these walls. I was seven years old at the time, and I thought, She has a putty face.) There was the library on lower High Street, above the Department of the Treasury, and it was in that part of High Street that all colonial government business took place. In that part of High Street, you could cash a cheque at the Treasury, read a book in the library, post a letter at the post office, appear before a magistrate in court. (Since we were ruled by the English, we also had their laws. There was a law against using abusive language. Can you imagine such a law among people for whom making a spectacle of yourself through speech is everything? When West Indians went to England, the police there had to get a glossary of bad West Indian words so they could understand whether they were hearing abusive language or not.) It was in that same part of High Street that you could get a passport in another government office. In the middle of High Street was the Barclays Bank. The Barclay brothers, who started Barclays Bank, were slave-traders. That is how they made their money. When the English outlawed the slave trade, the Barclay brothers went into banking. It made them even richer. It's possible that when they saw how rich banking made them, they gave themselves a good beating for opposing an end to slave trading (for surely they would have opposed that), but then again, they may have been visionaries and agitated for an end to slavery, for look at how rich they became with their banks borrowing from (through their savings) the descendants of the slaves and then lending back to them. But people just a little older than I am can recite the name of and the day the first black person was hired as a cashier at this very same Barclays Bank in Antigua. Do you ever wonder why some people blow things up? I can imagine that if my life had taken a certain turn, there would be the Barclays Bank, and there I would be, both of us in ashes. Do you ever try to understand why people like me cannot get over the past, cannot forgive and cannot forget? There is the Barclays Bank. The Barclay brothers are dead. The human beings they traded, the human beings who to them were only commodities, are dead. It should not have been that they came to the same end, and heaven is not enough of a reward for one or hell enough of a

punishment for the other. People who think about
these things believe that every bad deed, even every
bad thought, carries with it its own retribution. So
do you see the queer thing about people like me?
Sometimes we hold your retribution.

And then there was another place, called the
Mill Reef Club. It was built by some people from
North America who wanted to live in Antigua and
spend their holidays in Antigua but who seemed
not to like Antiguans (black people) at all, for the
Mill Reef Club declared itself completely private,
and the only Antiguans (black people) allowed to
go there were servants. People can recite the name
of the first Antiguan (black person) to eat a sand-
wich at the clubhouse and the day on which it
happened; people can recite the name of the first
Antiguan (black person) to play golf on the golf
course and the day on which the event took place.
In those days, we Antiguans thought that the people
at the Mill Reef Club had such bad manners, like
pigs; they were behaving in a bad way, like pigs.
There they were, strangers in someone else's home,
and then they refused to talk to their hosts or have
anything human, anything intimate, to do with
them. I believe they gave scholarships to one or
two bright people each year so they could go overseas and study; I believe they gave money to

children's charities; these things must have made
them seem to themselves very big and good, but to
us there they were, pigs living in that sty (the Mill
Reef Club). And what were these people from North
America, these people from England, these people
from Europe, with their bad behaviour, doing on
this little island? For they so enjoyed behaving
badly, as if there was pleasure immeasurable to be
had from not acting like a human being. Let me
tell you about a man; trained as a dentist, he took
it on himself to say he was a doctor, specialising in
treating children's illnesses. No one objected—cer-
tainly not us. He came to Antigua as a refugee
(running away from Hitler) from Czechoslovakia.
This man hated us so much that he would send his
wife to inspect us before we were admitted into his
presence, and she would make sure that we didn't
smell, that we didn't have dirt under our finger-
nails, and that nothing else about us—apart from
the colour of our skin—would offend the doctor. (I
can remember once, when I had whooping cough
and I took a turn for the worse, that my mother,
before bundling me up and taking me off to see
this man, examined me carefully to see that I had
no bad smells or dirt in the crease of my neck,
behind my ears, or anywhere else. Every horrible
thing that a housefly could do was known by heart

to my mother, and in her innocence she thought
that she and the doctor shared the same crazy obsession—germs.) Then there was a headmistress of a
girls' school, hired through the colonial office in
England and sent to Antigua to run this school
which only in my lifetime began to accept girls
who were born outside a marriage; in Antigua it
had never dawned on anyone that this was a way of
keeping black children out of this school. This
woman was twenty-six years old, not too long
out of university, from Northern Ireland, and she
told these girls over and over again to stop behaving
as if they were monkeys just out of trees. No one
ever dreamed that the word for any of this was
racism. We thought these people were so ill-
mannered and we were so surprised by this, for
they were far away from their home, and we be-
lieved that the farther away you were from your
home the better you should behave. (This is because
if your bad behaviour gets you in trouble you have
your family not too far off to help defend you.) We
thought they were un-Christian-like; we thought
they were small-minded; we thought they were like
animals, a bit below human standards as we understood those standards to be. We felt superior to all
these people; we thought that perhaps the English
among them who behaved this way weren't English

at all, for the English were supposed to be civilised, and this behaviour was so much like that of an animal, the thing we were before the English rescued us, that maybe they weren't from the real England at all but from another England, one we were not familiar with, not at all from the England we were told about, not at all from the England we could never be from, the England that was so far away, the England that not even a boat could take us to, the England that, no matter what we did, we could never be of. We felt superior, for we were so much better behaved and we were full of grace, and these people were so badly behaved and they were so completely empty of grace. (Of course, I now see that good behaviour is the proper posture of the weak, of children.) We were taught the names of the Kings of England. In Antigua, the twenty-fourth of May was a holiday—Queen Victoria's official birthday. We didn't say to ourselves, Hasn't this extremely unappealing person been dead for years and years? Instead, we were glad for a holiday. Once, at dinner (this happened in my present life), I was sitting across from an Englishman, one of those smart people who know how to run things that England still turns out but who now, since the demise of the empire, have nothing to do; they look so sad, sitting on the rubbish heap of history. I was reciting my usual litany of things I hold against England and the English, and to round things off I said, "And do you know that we had to celebrate Queen Victoria's birthday?" So he said that every year, at the school he attended in England, they marked the day she died. I said, "Well, apart from the fact that she belonged to you and so anything you did about her was proper, at least you knew she died." So that was England to us—Queen Victoria and the glorious day of her coming into the world, a beautiful place, a blessed place, a living and blessed thing, not the ugly, piggish individuals we met. I cannot tell you how angry it makes me to hear people from North America tell me how much they love England, how beautiful England is, with its traditions. All they see is some frumpy, wrinkled-up person passing by in a carriage waving at a crowd. But what I see is the millions of people, of whom I am just one, made orphans: no motherland, no fatherland, no gods, no mounds of earth for holy ground, no excess of love which might lead to the things that an excess of love sometimes brings, and worst and most painful of all, no tongue. (For isn't it odd that the only language I have in which to speak of this crime is the language of the criminal who committed the crime? And what can that really mean? For the language of the criminal can contain only the goodness of the criminal's deed. The language of the criminal can explain and express the deed only from the criminal's point of view. It cannot contain the horror of the deed, the injustice of the deed, the agony, the humiliation inflicted on me. When I say to the criminal, "This is wrong, this is wrong, this is wrong," or, "This deed is bad, and this other deed is bad, and this one is also very, very bad," the criminal understands the word "wrong" in this way: It is wrong when "he" doesn't get his fair share of profits from the crime just committed; he understands the word "bad" in this way: a fellow criminal betrayed a trust. That must be why, when I say, "I am filled with rage," the criminal says, "But why?" And when I blow things up and make life generally unlivable for the criminal (is my life not unlivable, too?) the criminal is shocked, surprised. But nothing can erase my rage—not an apology, not a large sum of money, not the death of the criminal—for this wrong can never be made right, and only the impossible can make me still: can a way be found to make what happened not have happened? And so look at this prolonged visit to the bile duct that I am making, look at how bitter, how dyspeptic just to sit and think about these things makes me. I attended a

school named after a Princess of England. Years
and years later, I read somewhere that this Princess
made her tour of the West Indies (which included
Antigua, and on that tour she dedicated my school)
because she had fallen in love with a married man,
and since she was not allowed to marry a divorced
man she was sent to visit us to get over her affair
with him. How well I remember that all of Antigua
turned out to see this Princess person, how every
building that she would enter was repaired and
painted so that it looked brand-new, how every
beach she would sun herself on had to look as if no
one had ever sunned there before (I wonder now
what they did about the poor sea? I mean, can a
sea be made to look brand-new?), and how everybody she met was the best Antiguan body to meet,
and no one told us that this person we were putting
ourselves out for on such a big scale, this person we
were getting worked up about as if she were God
Himself, was in our midst because of something
so common, so everyday: her life was not working
out the way she had hoped, her life was one big
mess. Have I given you the impression that the
Antigua I grew up in revolved almost completely
around England? Well, that was so. I met the world
through England, and if the world wanted to meet
me it would have to do so through England.

Are you saying to yourself, "Can't she get beyond all that, everything happened so long ago, and how does she know that if things had been the other way around her ancestors wouldn't have behaved just as badly, because, after all, doesn't everybody behave badly given the opportunity?"

Our perception of this Antigua—the perception we had of this place ruled by these bad-minded people—was not a political perception. The English were ill-mannered, not racists; the school head-mistress was especially ill-mannered, not a racist; the doctor was crazy—he didn't even speak English properly, and he came from a strangely named place, he also was not a racist; the people at the Mill Reef Club were puzzling (why go and live in a place populated mostly by people you cannot stand), not racists.

Have you ever wondered to yourself why it is that all people like me seem to have learned from you is how to imprison and murder each other, how to govern badly, and how to take the wealth of our country and place it in Swiss bank accounts? Have you ever wondered why it is that all we seem to have learned from you is how to corrupt our societies and how to be tyrants? You will have to accept that this is mostly your fault. Let me just show you how you looked to us. You came. You took things that were not yours, and you did not even, for appearances' sake, ask first. You could have said, "May I have this, please?" and even though it would have been clear to everybody that a yes or no from us would have been of no consequence you might have looked so much better. Believe me, it would have gone a long way. I would have had to admit that at least you were polite. You murdered people. You imprisoned people. You robbed people. You opened your own banks and you put our money in them. The accounts were in your name. The banks were in your name. There must have been some good people among you, but they stayed home. And that is the point. That is why they are good. They stayed home. But still, when you think about it, you must be a little sad. The people like me, finally, after years and years of agitation, made deeply moving and eloquent speeches against the wrongness of your domination over us, and then finally, after the mutilated bodies of you, your wife, and your children were found in your beautiful and spacious bungalow at the edge of your rubber plantation—found by one of your many house servants (none of it was ever yours; it was never, ever yours)—you say to me, "Well, I wash my hands of all of you, I am leaving now," and you leave, and from afar you watch as we do to ourselves the very things you used to do to us. And you might feel that there was more to you than that, you might feel that you had understood the meaning of the Age of Enlightenment (though, as far as I can see, it had done you very little good); you loved knowledge, and wherever you went you made sure to build a school, a library (yes, and in both of these places you distorted or erased my history and glorified your own). But then again, perhaps as you observe the debacle in which I now exist, the utter ruin that I say is my life, perhaps you are remembering that you had always felt people like me cannot run things, people like me will never grasp the idea of Gross National Product, people like me will never be able to take command of the thing the most simpleminded among you can master, people like me will never understand the notion of rule by law, people like me cannot really think in abstractions, people like me cannot be objective, we make everything so personal. You will forget your part in the whole setup, that bureaucracy is one of your inventions, that Gross National Product is one of your inventions, and all the laws that you know mysteriously favour you. Do you know why people like me are shy about being capitalists? Well, it's because we, for as long as we have known you, *were* capital, like bales of cotton and sacks of sugar, and you were the commanding, cruel capitalists, and the memory of this is so strong, the experience so recent, that we can't quite bring ourselves to embrace this idea that you think so much of. As for what we were like before we met you, I no longer care. No periods of time over which my ancestors held sway, no documentation of complex civilisations, is any comfort to me. Even if I really came from people who were living like monkeys in trees, it was better to be that than what happened to me, what I became after I met you.

A N D S O Y O U can imagine how I felt when, one day, in Antigua, standing on Market Street, looking up one way and down the other, I asked myself: Is the Antigua I see before me, self-ruled, a worse place than what it was when it was dominated by the bad-minded English and all the bad-minded things they brought with them? How did Antigua get to such a state that I would have to ask myself this? For the answer on every Antiguan's lips to the question "What is going on here now?" is "The government is corrupt. Them are thief, them are big thief." Imagine, then, the bitterness and the shame in me as I tell you this. I was standing on Market Street in front of the library. The library! But why is the library on Market Street? I had asked myself.

Why is the old building that was damaged in the
famous earthquake years ago, the building that has
the legend on it THIS BUILDING WAS DAMAGED IN THE
EARTHQUAKE OF 1974. REPAIRS ARE PENDING, not
repaired and the library put back in the place where
it used to be? Or, why, years after The Earthquake
damaged the old library building, has a new library
not been built? Why is the library above a dry-
goods store in an old run-down cement-brick building? Oh, you might be saying to yourself, Why is
she so undone at what has become of the library,
why does she think that is a good example of corruption, of things gone bad? But if you saw the old
library, situated as it was, in a big, old wooden
building painted a shade of yellow that is beautiful
to people like me, with its wide veranda, its big,
always open windows, its rows and rows of shelves
filled with books, its beautiful wooden tables and
chairs for sitting and reading, if you could hear the
sound of its quietness (for the quiet in this library
was a sound in itself), the smell of the sea (which
was a stone's throw away), the heat of the sun (no
building could protect us from that), the beauty of
us sitting there like communicants at an altar,
taking in, again and again, the fairy tale of how we
met you, your right to do the things you did, how
beautiful you were, are, and always will be; if you

42

could see all of that in just one glimpse, you would see why my heart would break at the dung heap that now passes for a library in Antigua. The place where the library is now, above the dry-goods store, in the old run-down concrete building, is too small to hold all the books from the old building, and so most of the books, instead of being on their nice shelves, resting comfortably, waiting to acquaint me with you in all your greatness, are in cardboard boxes in a room, gathering mildew, or dust, or ruin. In this place, the young librarians cannot find the things they want, and I don't know whether it is because of the chaos of storing for a long period of time the contents of a public library in cardboard boxes, or because of the bad post-colonial education the young librarians have received. (In Antigua today, most young people seem almost illiterate. On the airwaves, where they work as news personalities, they speak English as if it were their sixth language. Once, I attended an event at carnival time called a "Teenage Pageant." In this event, teenagers, male and female, paraded around on a stadium stage, singing pop songs—a hideous song called "The Greatest Love" was a particular favourite among them to perform—reciting poems they had written about slavery—there is an appropriate obsession with slavery—and generally making asses of

43

themselves. What surprised me most about them was not how familiar they were with the rubbish of North America—compared to the young people of my generation, who were familiar with the rubbish of England—but, unlike my generation, how stupid they seemed, how unable they were to answer in a straightforward way, and in their native tongue of English, simple questions about themselves. In my generation, they would not have been allowed on the school stage, much less before an audience in a stadium.) The head librarian, the same one from colonial days, seemed to spend her time wondering if there was anybody with money or influence to help the library, apologising to people—Antiguans returning to Antigua after a long absence—who are shocked and offended by the sight of the library sitting on top of a dry-goods store, wondering if in the end the people at the Mill Reef Club will relent and contribute their money to the building of a new library, instead of holding to their repair-of-the-old-library-or-nothing position. (The people at the Mill Reef Club love the old Antigua. I love the old Antigua. Without question, we don't have the same old Antigua in mind.) When I was growing up and was a member of the library, this woman was the head librarian. In those days, she seemed imperious and stuck-up,

suspicious of us (in my case, she was justified; I
stole many books from this library. I didn't mean to
steal the books, really; it's just that once I had read
a book I couldn't bear to part with it), always sure
that we meant to do some bad. She must have been
very proud of her work then and her association
with such an institution, for, to see her now, she
looks the opposite of her old self. I would go to that
library every Saturday afternoon—the last stop on
my Saturday-afternoon round of things to do (I
would save this for last, for it was the thing I liked
to do best)—and sit and look at books and think
about the misery in being me (I was a child and
what is a child if not someone full of herself or
himself), whom I loved, whom I did not love,
whom I only just liked, and so on. I think that by
around nine years of age I had read all the books
in the children's section (it was a very small collec-
tion), and so I had to use my mother's library card
to borrow books from the adult section. It is this
same librarian who now stands over the shame of
what is now the library who used to watch me
closely, trying to make sure that I didn't leave the
library with more books than I was allowed, and
leave with them in such a way that meant they
would never be seen in any library but my own
again. This woman kept a close watch on me,

making sure that I didn't walk out with books held
tightly between my legs (what a trick, I thought)
or in the basket that I carried to hold my Saturday-
afternoon purchases. And so again, can you see
why it is that the library might mean something
to me, why it might make me feel sad to see it
reduced to its present condition? For at the moment
that I was standing on Market Street and looking
up at the thing called the library, the old building
where the library used to be was occupied by, and
served as headquarters for, a carnival troupe. The
theme of this carnival troupe was "Angels from the
Realm," and it seemed to me that there was something in that, though not a deliberate something,
just a something, like an "Angels from the Realm
of Innocence" something. (And I supposed it made
sense for something from the realm of culture to
occupy a building that used to house something
from the realm of education, for in Antigua, the
Minister of Education is also the Minister of Culture.) Where the shelves of books used to be, where
the wooden tables and chairs used to be, where the
sound of quietness used to be, where the smell of
the sea used to be, where everything used to be, was
now occupied by costumes: costumes for angels
from the realm. Some of the costumes were for angels before the Fall, some of the costumes were for

angels after the Fall; the ones representing After the Fall were the best. And so what sort of place has Antigua become that the people from the Mill Reef Club are allowed a say in anything? That they are allowed to live there the way they continue to live there is bad enough. I then went to see a woman whose family had helped to establish the Mill Reef Club. She had been mentioned to me as someone who was very active in getting the old library restored. I knew of this woman, for she is notorious for liking Antiguans only if they are servants. After I mentioned the library to her, the first thing she told me was that she always encouraged her girls and her girls' children to use the library, and by her girls she meant grownup Antiguan women (not unlike me) who work in her gift shop as seamstresses and saleswomen. She said to me then what everybody in Antigua says sooner or later: The government is for sale; anybody from anywhere can come to Antigua and for a sum of money can get what he wants. And I had to ask myself, What exactly should I feel toward the people who robbed me of the right to make a reply to this woman? For I could see the pleasure she took in pointing out to me the gutter into which a self-governing—black— Antigua had placed itself. In any case, this woman and her friends at the Mill Reef Club wanted to restore the old library, but she said she didn't know if they would be able to do so, because that part of St. John's was going to be developed, turned into little shops—boutiques—so that when tourists turned up they could buy all those awful things that tourists always buy, all those awful things they then take home, put in their attics, and their children have to throw out when the tourists, finally, die. I had heard from many people that the person who wanted to develop that part of St. John's was a foreigner, who was once wanted in the Far East for swindling a government out of oil profits, a man so notorious that he cannot travel with a passport from the country of which he is a citizen but travels on a diplomatic passport issued by the government of Antigua. I thought, then, that I should ask the Minister of Education about the library. I am sure he would have had a good explanation for why it is that for so many years this island, which has as its motto of Independence "A People to Mold, A Nation to Build" has not had a proper library, but at the moment that I wanted to ask him this question he was in Trinidad attending a cricket match, something he must have been bound to do, since he is not only the Minister of Education and the Minister of Culture but also the Minister of

Sport. In Antigua, cricket is sport and cricket is culture. (But let me just tell you something about Ministers of Culture: in places where there is a Minister of Culture it means there is no culture. For have you ever heard of any culture springing up under the umbrella of a Minister of Culture? Countries with Ministers of Culture must be like countries with Liberty Weekend. Do you remember Liberty Weekend? In the week before Liberty Weekend, the United States Supreme Court ruled that ordinary grown-up people could not do as they pleased behind the locked doors of their own bedroom. I would have thought, then, that the people whose idea it was to have the Liberty Weekend business would have been so ashamed at such a repudiation of liberty that they would have cancelled the whole thing. But not at all; and so in a country that had less liberty than it used to have, Liberty Weekend was celebrated. In countries that have no culture or are afraid they may have no culture, there is a Minister of Culture. And what is culture, anyway? In some places, it's the way they play drums; in other places, it's the way you behave out in public; and in still other places, it's just the way a person cooks food. And so what is there to preserve about these things? For is it not so that people make them up as they go along, make them up as they need them?) Oh, I suppose that it was just as well that the Minister of Culture was not in Antigua then, for I did not know how this man would take to me or anything I might say. It so happens that in Antigua my mother is fairly notorious for her political opinions. She is almost painfully frank, quite unable to keep any thoughts she has about anything—and she has many thoughts on almost everything—to herself. My mother, at one time, was a supporter of the second successful political party Antigua has ever had. In the years that Antiguans have been electing governments, only once have they elected a political party other than the party now in power. In one election campaign, my mother was putting up her party's posters on a lamppost just outside the house of the Minister of Culture. When the minister, hearing a great hubbub (my mother would only do this with a great hubbub) came outside and saw that it was my mother, he said, perhaps to the air, "What is *she* doing here?" And to this my mother replied, "I may be a she, but I am a good she. Not someone who steals stamps from Redonda." Whatever this meant to the Minister of Culture my mother would not tell me, but it made the minister turn and go back inside his house without a reply. Redonda is a

barren rock out in the Caribbean Sea—actually
closer to the islands of Montserrat and Nevis than
to Antigua, but for reasons known only to the
English person who did this, Redonda and the
islands of Barbuda and Antigua are all lumped
together as one country. When Antiguans talk about
"The Nation" (and they say "The Nation" without irony), they are referring to the nine-by-twelve-
mile-long, drought-ridden island of Antigua; they
are referring to Barbuda, an island even smaller
than Antigua (Barbuda was settled originally by a
family from England named Condrington; this
family specialised in breeding special groups of
black people, whom they then sold into slavery);
and they are referring to a barren little rock,
where only booby birds live, Redonda. Once there
was a scandal about stamps issued for Redonda.
A lot of money was made on these stamps, but
no one seems to know who got the money or
where the stamps actually ended up. Where do all
these stamps, in all their colourfulness, where do
they come from? I mean, whose idea is it? Antigua
has no stamp designer on the government payroll;
there is no building that houses the dyes and the
paper on which the stamps are printed; there is no
Department of Printing. So who decides to print

stamps celebrating the Queen of England's birthday? Who decides to celebrate Mickey Mouse's
birthday? Who decides that stamps from this part
of the world should be colourful and bright and not
sedate and subdued, like, say, a stamp from Canada?
I suppose that somewhere there is a stamp syndicate
and that from time to time its people decide what
would be best for the syndicate's financial interest,
and they issue these stamps to these poor sap
countries like Antigua.

In a small place, people cultivate small events.
The small event is isolated, blown up, turned over
and over, and then absorbed into the everyday, so
that at any moment it can and will roll off the
inhabitants of the small place's tongues. For the
people in a small place, every event is a domestic
event; the people in a small place cannot see themselves in a larger picture, they cannot see that they
might be part of a chain of something, anything.
The people in a small place see the event in the
distance heading directly towards them and they
say, "I see the thing and it is heading towards me."
The people in a small place then experience the
event as if it were sitting on top of their heads, their

shoulders, and it weighs them down, this enormous
burden that is the event, so that they cannot breathe
properly and they cannot think properly and they
say, "This thing that was only coming towards me
is now on top of me," and they live like that, until
eventually they absorb the event and it becomes a
part of them, a part of who and what they really
are, and they are complete in that way until another
event comes along and the process begins again.

The people in a small place cannot give an
exact account, a complete account, of themselves.
The people in a small place cannot give an exact account, a complete account of events (small
though they may be). This cannot be held against
them; an exact account, a complete account, of anything, anywhere, is not possible. (The hour in the
day, the day of the year some ships set sail is a
small, small detail in any picture, any story; but
the picture itself, the story itself depend on things
that can never, ever be pinned down.) The people
in a small place can have no interest in the exact,
or in completeness, for that would demand a careful
weighing, careful consideration, careful judging,
careful questioning. It would demand the invention
of a silence, inside of which these things could be
done. It would demand a reconsideration, an ad-

justment, in the way they understand the existence of Time. To the people in a small place, the division of Time into the Past, the Present, and the Future does not exist. An event that occurred one hundred years ago might be as vivid to them as if it were happening at this very moment. And then, an event that is occurring at this very moment might pass before them with such dimness that it is as if it had happened one hundred years ago. No action in the present is an action planned with a view of its effect on the future. When the future, bearing its own events, arrives, its ancestry is then traced in a trancelike retrospect, at the end of which, their mouths and eyes wide with their astonishment, the people in a small place reveal themselves to be like children being shown the secrets of a magic trick.

In Antigua, people speak of slavery as if it had been a pageant full of large ships sailing on blue water, the large ships filled up with human cargo— their ancestors; they got off, they were forced to work under conditions that were cruel and in- human, they were beaten, they were murdered, they were sold, their children were taken from them and these separations lasted forever, there were many other bad things, and then suddenly the whole thing came to an end in something called emancipation. Then they speak of emancipation itself as if it happened just the other day, not over one hundred and fifty years ago. The word "emancipation" is used so frequently, it is as if it, emancipation, were a contemporary occurrence, something everybody is familiar with. And perhaps there is something in that, for an institution that is often celebrated in Antigua is the Hotel Training School, a school that teaches Antiguans how to be good servants, how to be a good nobody, which is what a servant is. In Antigua, people cannot see a relationship between their obsession with slavery and emancipation and their celebration of the Hotel Training School (graduation ceremonies are broadcast on radio and television); people cannot see a relationship between their obsession with slavery and emancipation and the fact that they are governed by corrupt men, or that these corrupt men have given their country away to corrupt foreigners. The men who rule Antigua came to power in open, free elections. In accounts of the capture and enslavement of black people almost no slave ever mentions who captured and delivered him or her to the European master. In accounts of their corrupt government, Antiguans neglect to say that in twenty years of one form of self-government or another, they have, with one five-year exception, placed in power the present government.

Antigua is a small place. Antigua is a very small place. In Antigua, not only is the event turned into everyday but the everyday is turned into an event. (Here is this: On a Saturday, at market, two people who, as far as they know, have never met before, collide by accident; this accidental collision leads to an enormous quarrel—a drama, really—in which the two people stand at opposite ends of a street and shout insults at each other at the top of their lungs. This event soon becomes everyday, for every time these two people meet each other again, sometimes by accident, sometimes by design, the shouting and the insults begin.) But event turned into everyday and everyday turned into event do not remain event and everyday, in a fixed state. They go back and forth, exchanging places, and their status from day to day depends on all sorts of internal shadings and internal colourings, and the forces that manipulate these internal shadings and internal colourings are kept deliberately mysterious and unknown. And might not knowing why they are the way they are, why they do the things they do, why they live the way they live and in the place they live, why the things that happened to them happened, lead these people to a different relation-

ship with the world, a more demanding relationship, a relationship in which they are not victims
all the time of every bad idea that flits across the
mind of the world? And might not knowing why
they are the way they are and why they do the
things they do put in their proper place everyday
and event, so that exceptional amounts of energy
aren't expended on the trivial, while the substan-
tial and the important are assembled (artfully)
into a picture story ("He did this and then he
did that")? I look at this place (Antigua), I look
at these people (Antiguans), and I cannot tell
whether I was brought up by, and so come from,
children, eternal innocents, or artists who have
not yet found eminence in a world too stupid to
understand, or lunatics who have made their own
lunatic asylum, or an exquisite combination of
all three.

For it is in a voice that suggests all three that
they say: "That big new hotel is a haven for drug
dealing. The hotel has its own port of entry, so
boats bearing their drug cargo can come and go as
they please. The bay where the new hotel is situated
used to have the best wilks in the world, but where
did they all go? Even though all the beaches in Antigua are by law public beaches, Antiguans are not
allowed on the beaches of this hotel; they are stopped

at the gate by guards; and soon the best beaches in Antigua will be closed to Antiguans. A Japanese-car dealership, one of the largest Japanese-car dealerships between the borders of Canada and South America, bears the name of a Syrian national, but some of the ministers in government own shares in it, and that is why all government vehicles are that particular brand of Japanese-made vehicle. All the customs inspectors have as their private vehicle that particular brand of Japanese-made car, and a luxurious model, at that. Every year, the customs inspectors get the latest models. Some other ministers in government have also gone into the Japanese-car import business; and if they someday find themselves in the right position, they will change the government's vehicles to the make of Japanese vehicle that their company imports. The utility poles not only hold the electric and telephone wiring that utility poles usually hold; they also carry the heavier wiring for cable television. The electric and telephone services are owned by the government. The cable-television service is owned by a minister in government, a son of the Prime Minister. The utility poles are old and rotten, and they sag and then fall down under the weight of the wires and cables. When they fall down, the government replaces them with new ones, and at no cost to the owner of the cable-television franchise. Some ministers in government have opened their own businesses; the main customer for these businesses is the government itself; the government then declares that only that company can be licenced to import the commodity that the business sells; great effort goes into concealing who the owners of these businesses are. People close to the Prime Minister openly run one of the largest houses of prostitution in Antigua. Some offshore banks are fronts for bad people hiding money acquired through dealings in drugs, or the other bad ways there are to acquire money, though it seems to be true that in Antigua all the ways there are to acquire large sums of money are bad ways. It is not a secret that a minister is involved in drug trafficking. That minister and another minister in government benefit from the offshore banks, with their ill-gotten deposits. (These offshore banks are popular in the West Indies. Only tourism itself is more important. Every government wants to have these banks, which are modelled on the banks in Switzerland. I have a friend who just came back from Switzerland. What a wonderful time she had. She had never seen cleaner streets anywhere, or more wonderful people anywhere. She was in such a rhapsodic state about the Swiss, and the superior life they lead, that it was hard for me not to bring up how they must pay for this superior life they lead. For almost not a day goes by that I don't hear about some dictator, some tyrant from somewhere in the world, who has robbed his country's treasury, stolen the aid from foreign governments, and placed it in his own personal and secret Swiss bank account; not a day goes by that I don't hear of some criminal kingpin, some investor, who has a secret Swiss bank account. But maybe there is no connection between the wonderful life that the Swiss lead and the ill-gotten money that is resting in Swiss bank vaults; maybe it's just a coincidence. The Swiss are famous for their banking system and for making superior timepieces. Switzerland is a neutral country, money is a neutral commodity, and time is neutral, too, being neither here nor there, one thing or another.) Some gambling casinos in the hotels are controlled by mobsters from the United States. They pay somebody in government who allows them to operate. If they benefit from the operation of these casinos, they—people in Antigua—cannot see in what way, except for the seasonal employment it offers a few people, for, after all, all government services are bad. (Gambling, linked here completely to tourism, is another popular industry in the West

Indies. Every government in the West Indies seems to want hotels with gambling casinos. It would appear that nobody wants to go to the West Indies without being able to spend time in a gambling casino. I once heard a semiliterate-sounding man on Radio Montserrat berating people, mostly clergymen, who were opposed to the opening of gambling casinos on the island of Montserrat. He said that when the people of Montserrat were hungry, they didn't look to the church for food, or to those other people who opposed the casinos, they looked to the government, and so he had to find a way to feed them. It's possible that if someone had told him that the operation of gambling casinos in hotels in the West Indies seems to feed, in a very big way, everybody connected with them, except for the people he had in mind, it might have given him pause. I do not know. At the end of the program the announcer identified this man as the head of government of Montserrat.) The government of Antigua allowed some special ammunition to be tested in Antigua—ammunition that the government knew very well was to be shipped to the government of South Africa. The government allowed meat known to be contaminated by radiation to be distributed in Antigua. A food importer, a man from an old Antiguan family, regularly lends the government money. How does a food importer on a small island have enough money to lend to a government? Syrian and Lebanese nationals regularly lend the government money. Syrian and Lebanese nationals own large amounts of land in Antigua, and on the land they own in the countryside they build condominiums that they then sell (prices quoted in United States dollars) to North Americans and Europeans. (The condominium style of building, ugly in any climate, is especially ugly in a small, hot place. Imagine these concrete, box-like structures, stacked against each other as if they were tinned goods in a store with not enough shelf space, overlooking an expanse of three different shades of blue seawater. It's true—condominiums degrade everything around them.) The Syrians and Lebanese own large amounts of commercial property in Antigua. They build large concrete buildings, and then the government of Antigua rents all the space in these buildings. Why can't the government of Antigua build its own government buildings? What is the real interest paid on these loans made to the government? And are the loans made to the government or are they really made to persons in the government but charged to the government? What is the real rent paid to the Syrian and Lebanese landlords, for no one believes the sum

quoted, even though it is quite high; for some of
the spaces rented, the rent already paid could have
bought the building (the library on Market Street)
many times over. In the Antigua telephone direc-
tory, the Syrians and Lebanese have more business
addresses and telephone numbers than any of the
other same surnames listed. Antigua's Ambassador
to Syria is a member of a Syrian family. It makes
sense. He speaks Syrian. But why does Antigua need
an ambassador to Syria? The Syrians and Lebanese
are called "those foreigners" even though most of
them have acquired Antiguan citizenship. North
Americans and Europeans are not foreigners; they
are white people. Everybody is used to white people.
The Syrians and Lebanese are not "white people."
They have no cultural institutions in Antigua—not
even a restaurant. The Syrians and the Lebanese
look as if they know that at any time they could be
asked to leave, and perhaps they are right, for who
knows how everything will turn out? A calypso
singer's sister's body was found, with the head
chopped off, near the island's United States Army
base. To this day, no one has been charged with
this murder. A European woman was found
murdered in her home out at Freeman's Village.
No one has been charged with this murder. A man,
a government official who was gathering evidence

of financial wrongdoing by the government, was electrocuted when he went to his refrigerator to get himself a drink. His son, who came into the kitchen and found his father's body stuck to the refrigerator, was electrocuted, too, when he grabbed his father and tried to remove him. Father and son were given a double funeral, and practically all of Antigua turned out either as mourners or as observers of the mourners. No one can understand, to this day, how an ordinary refrigerator can electrocute someone who opens the door, unless it was fixed to electrocute someone who opened the door. In the months that lead up to carnival, the Governor General, a very stuck-up man, with an even more stuck-up wife, or a very ordinary sort of man whose wife does her own shopping at the supermarket, goes to England. The house in which he lives, Government House, is right across from the grounds where carnival events are held, and he goes to England because he can't stand the noise. When he is away, the Prime Minister names a person, another man, to be Acting Governor General. This man is usually someone connected to the Prime Minister's party. One year, the man who was Acting Governor General died while taking an afternoon swim in the swimming pool of one of the Syrian nationals. This man and the Syrian nationals were very good friends. He was a shareholder in their Japanese-car company. He was the one who had first brought them into government schemes. He died while swimming in this swimming pool. The Syrians had suffered a series of break-ins and robberies, and they had their house wired with live wires, so that if someone broke in, the intruder would be electrocuted; they had forgotten to turn off the wire leading to or around the swimming pool, and the Acting Governor General was electrocuted. Lying in his coffin, he looked black, as if he had been scorched from the inside. His funeral was practically a pageant, and Antigua had never seen anything like it. The man who succeeded him, the second Acting Governor General in two months, got sick at this funeral. He said he felt sick. He vomited. He was taken home in a car; then he got better. While attending the funeral of another big person, he fainted. He vomited. Doctors, attending the funeral as ordinary mourners, said there was nothing really wrong, but just to be sure, they looked at him, had him admitted to hospital. (The hospital in Antigua is so dirty, so run-down, that even if the best doctors and nurses in the world were employed, a person from another part of the world—Europe or North America—would not feel confident leaving a domestic animal there.) The doctors said there was nothing wrong with him, but just to make sure, just to be on the safe side, he was placed in Intensive Care. The Intensive Care part of the hospital is the only part of the hospital that would inspire confidence in a sick person, and for a man as prominent as he was that was the only thing to do. His friends visited him in the hospital. He told jokes. They laughed. They said, "See you tomorrow." They left him. He died. They were surprised, because he had seemed his old self. It was his heart; he had had a heart problem. He was poisoned; how can your heart make you vomit and froth at the mouth and fall down in a stupor and then revive and go on as before? Twice, he got sick at funerals, so it must have been something he ate. Bradley Carrot (the name of the third Acting Governor General in two months) is looking over his shoulder. All of the ministers in government go overseas for medical treatment. Not one of them would stay in the hospital here.

Eleven million dollars that the French government gave to the Antiguan government for developmental aid has vanished. A high government official got millions of dollars in bribes for allowing a particular kind of industrial plant to be built. The salt floating around in the Antiguan air soon caused the plant to rust. All the airwaves in Antigua are owned

by the government or ministers in government.
On the airwaves, the opposition parties are never
mentioned except to denounce them and to say
that they are Communists and that they have
received money from Fidel Castro and Muammar
Qaddafi. Antigua was going to have an oil-
refining industry. West Indies Oil, it was going
to be called. The government built the big tanks
to hold the oil before it was refined and the oil
after it was refined. They built a platform far out
at sea, where the large tankers would load and un-
load the cargo. The government built a refinery.
Something went wrong. The refinery is rusting. The
tanks are rusting. The platform is rusting. The foreigner who did the bad things in the Far East was involved in this. He is not rusting. He is very rich and
travels the world on a diplomatic passport issued to
him by the government of Antigua. He has more
plans. He wants to build for the people of Antigua
a museum and a library. The papers of the slave-
trading family from Barbuda (the Condringtons),
the records of their traffic in human lives, were
being auctioned. The government of Antigua made
a bid for them. Someone else made a larger bid.
He was the foreigner. His bid was the successful
bid. He then made a gift of these papers to
the people of Antigua. And what does it mean?

The records of one set of enemies, bought by another enemy, given to the people who have been their victims as a gift. The people who go into running the government were not always such big thieves; nor have they always been so corrupt. They took things, but it was on a small scale. For instance, if the government built some new housing to be sold to people, then a minister or two would get a few of the houses for themselves. They would then sell them outright, or rent them. Everybody knew about this. Some of the ministers were honest. One of them, a famous one in Antigua, a leader of the Trade and Labour Union movement, even died a pauper. Another minister, when his party lost power, had to drive a taxi. It is he, the taxi-driving ex-minister, who taught the other ministers a lesson. If you say to them, "Why you all so thief?" they say, "When I leave here, you want me to go drive taxi?" All the ministers have "green cards"—a document that makes them legal residents of the United States of America. The ministers, the people who govern the island of Antigua, who are also citizens of Antigua, are legal residents of the United States, a place they visit frequently.

And it is in that strange voice, then—the voice that suggests innocence, art, lunacy—that they say these things, pausing to take breath before this

monument to rottenness, that monument to rottenness, as if they were tour guides; as if, having ob-
served the event of tourism, they have absorbed it so
completely that they have made the degradation
and humiliation of their daily lives into their own
tourist attraction.

An event in Antigua has been the founding, in
1939, of the Antigua Trades and Labour Union, an
organization whose purpose was to obtain better
wages, better working conditions, and just a better
life in general for working people in Antigua. It
eventually became, along with being a union, a
political party, demanding universal suffrage, demanding that land in Antigua not be owned by
syndicates made up of English people (most of
whom still lived in England and had never laid eyes
on Antigua), but by Antiguans, and demanding
that Antiguans rule Antigua. An event in Antigua
has been that the president of this union has headed
the government in Antigua, as Premier and then,
when Antigua became independent from Britain, as
Prime Minister, for twenty-five of the thirty years
that Antigua had had some form of self-government.
Sometimes, when Antiguans look at this man, they
see the event of George Washington, liberator and

first President of the United States; sometimes, when Antiguans look at this man, they see the event of Jackie Presser, the head of the Teamsters Union in America, who is now serving time in prison for misappropriating his union's funds. For five years, Antigua had another Prime Minister. He stood for but was not re-elected to that office. The Prime Minister whose reign he interrupted then had him charged with using his office for personal profit, and he was sent to jail for eight months. The event of the Prime Minister whose career ended in political defeat and then jail is a sad event, for people had hoped that he would replace the old, dull, corrupt event with honesty, brilliance, and prosperity; instead, the sugar industry went bankrupt, the tourists did not come, his Minister of Public Works was dismissed because he was thought to have taken large amounts of public money, his illegitimate half brother, a member of his cabinet, spat on a stewardess while an aeroplane on which he was a passenger was in flight.

The event of the corruptness of the other Prime Minister of Antigua is traced to another event. They say that when this Prime Minister was a young man he worked for a merchant-importer who was also one of the largest bakers in Antigua. He worked for this man as a bookkeeper, and as a young bookkeeper he earned a salary that a young bookkeeper would earn, but the merchant-importer noticed that this young bookkeeper owned brand-new motorcars and seemed generally prosperous. In Antigua and in the 1930s, very few people owned cars or were generally prosperous, so the merchant-importer asked to look at his books. Whatever was wrong with the books the young man did not want the merchant-importer to see, for he took the books and ran with them to the bakery, and, with his incredibly long arms, he threw them into the furnace, where they perished immediately, never to be seen by mortal eyes again. And so they anchor the merchant-importer's books being burned to the event of the original, honest leaders of the Antigua Trades and Labour Union being maneuvered out of the union they founded and dishonest people taking their place; and they anchor that to the decline of one sort of colonialism and its debasement and its own sort of corruption; and they anchor that to this man, this Prime Minister, who from time to time had seemed like a good man, so well could he spell out the predicament that average Antiguans found themselves in. They anchor all of that to this other event: In Antigua, when a man goes into business, he will put up a sign announcing it, and on the sign he states the sort of business he is open to conducting

and he states his own name, followed by the words
& SON, so that it might read this way: DAVID A. DREW
& SON, CABINETMAKER AND CARPENTER. In Antigua,
people say that the man who has headed the government for twenty-five years perhaps by now thinks
that the government of Antigua is his own business,
for two of his sons are members of his cabinet,
holding the most important posts after the post of
Prime Minister. They are in charge of the Treasury,
Tourism, Public Works—departments of government through which large amounts of money pass.
And after they look at the father and the sons, they
say, What next? for it occurs to them that a family
that has been wielding political power for so many
years might not give it up easily, might not give it
up if they find themselves defeated at the polls,
might not let themselves be defeated at the polls,
might not even allow any polls. They note that
Antigua has an army of sorts, an army that can
only stand around as a decoration, the way it did
in Grenada when the United States invaded that
island; an army, then, that can only lend legitimacy
to illegitimate acts. And though this army cannot
really fight a war, is not trained to really fight a
war—Antigua, after all, has no enemies—the men
in this army can shoot at people, and if they cannot
fight a war but can shoot at people, what people will

they shoot at? And so people see anchored to this father and his two sons who have wielded power in Antigua for so many years, and who might find it hard to quietly relinquish this power and sit in New York spending the contents of their enormous bank accounts, the event of Haiti and the Duvaliers. The father, they say, is old and weak, and needs daily injections of powerful things to keep him going. They point, then, to one of the sons. They say how much they are reminded of Baby Doc and the opulent and fun-filled life he led in his poverty-stricken country. And they point to the other son and say that they are reminded of Papa Doc himself, for he is the ruthless son, the one who is not afraid of anything, the one who won't resign his post in government, even though he has been unable to account for large sums of money for public-works projects. But then, sitting with the prospect of that event facing them, they, Antiguans, say, perhaps not, perhaps that event will not be the event to take place, because the Baby Doc-like son who loves opulence and fun really loves opulence and fun, and like Baby Doc, he is not really a leader at all; and the other son, the Papa Doc-like son, is dying of leukemia or some other dreadful blood disease and has to go to New York every month for treatment. And so then they imagine another

73

event, the event of Maurice Bishop in Grenada, and they imagine that such a man will materialise in Antigua and he'll do Maurice Bishop-like things and say Maurice Bishop-like things and come to a Maurice Bishop-like end—death, only this time at the hands of the Americans.

ANTIGUA is beautiful. Antigua is too beautiful. Sometimes the beauty of it seems unreal. Sometimes the beauty of it seems as if it were stage sets for a play, for no real sunset could look like that; no real seawater could strike that many shades of blue at once; no real sky could be that shade of blue—another shade of blue, completely different from the shades of blue seen in the sea—and no real cloud could be that white and float just that way in that blue sky; no real day could be that sort of sunny and bright, making everything seem transparent and shallow; and no real night could be that sort of black, making everything seem thick and deep and bottomless. No real day and no real night could be that evenly divided—twelve hours of one and twelve hours of the other; no real day would begin that dramatically or end that dramatically (there is no dawn in Antigua: one minute, you are in the complete darkness of night; the next minute, the sun is overhead and it stays there until it sets with an explosion of reds on the horizon, and then the darkness of night comes again, and it is as if the open lid of a box you are inside suddenly snaps into place). No real sand on any real shore is that fine or that white (in some places) or that pink (in other places); no real flowers could be these shades of red, purple, yellow, orange, blue, white; no real lily would bloom only at night and perfume the air with a sweetness so thick it makes you slightly sick; no real earth is that colour brown; no real grass is that particular shade of dilapidated, run-down green (not enough rain); no real cows look that poorly as they feed on the unreal-looking grass in the unreal-looking pasture, and no real cows look quite that miserable as some unreal-looking white egrets sit on their backs eating insects; no real rain would fall with that much force, so that it tears up the parched earth. No real village in any real countryside would be named Table Hill Gordon, and no real village with such a name would be so beautiful in its pauperedness, its simpleness, its one-room houses painted in unreal shades of pink and yellow and green, a dog asleep in the shade, some flies asleep in the corner of the dog's mouth. Or the market on a Saturday morning, where the colours of the fruits and vegetables and the colours of the clothes people are wearing and the colour of the day itself, and the colour of the nearby sea, and the colour of the sky, which is just overhead and seems so close you might reach up and touch it, and the way the people there speak English (they break it up) and the way they might be angry with each other and the sound they make when they laugh, all of this is so beautiful, all of this is not real like any other real thing that there is. It is as if, then, the beauty—the beauty of the sea, the land, the air, the trees, the market, the people, the sounds they make—were a prison, and as if everything and everybody inside it were locked in and everything and everybody that is not inside it were locked out. And what might it do to ordinary people to live in this way every day? What might it do to them to live in such heightened, intense surroundings day after day? They have nothing to compare this incredible constant with, no big historical moment to compare the way they are now to the way they used to be. No Industrial Revolution, no revolution of any kind, no Age of Anything, no world wars, no decades of turbulence balanced by decades of calm.

Nothing, then, natural or unnatural, to leave a mark on their character. It is just a little island. The unreal way in which it is beautiful now is the unreal way in which it was always beautiful. The unreal way in which it is beautiful now that they are a free people is the unreal way in which it was beautiful when they were slaves.

Again, Antigua is a small place, a small island. It is nine miles wide by twelve miles long. It was discovered by Christopher Columbus in 1493. Not too long after, it was settled by human rubbish from Europe, who used enslaved but noble and exalted human beings from Africa (all masters of every stripe are rubbish, and all slaves of every stripe are noble and exalted; there can be no question about this) to satisfy their desire for wealth and power, to feel better about their own miserable existence, so that they could be less lonely and empty—a European disease. Eventually, the masters left, in a kind of way; eventually, the slaves were freed, in a kind of way. The people in Antigua now, the people who really think of themselves as Antiguans (and the people who would immediately come to your mind when you think about what Antiguans might be like; I mean, supposing you were to think about it), are the descendants of those noble and exalted people, the slaves. Of course, the whole thing is, once you cease to be a master, once you throw off your master's yoke, you are no longer human rubbish, you are just a human being, and all the things that adds up to. So, too, with the slaves. Once they are no longer slaves, once they are free, they are no longer noble and exalted; they are just human beings.